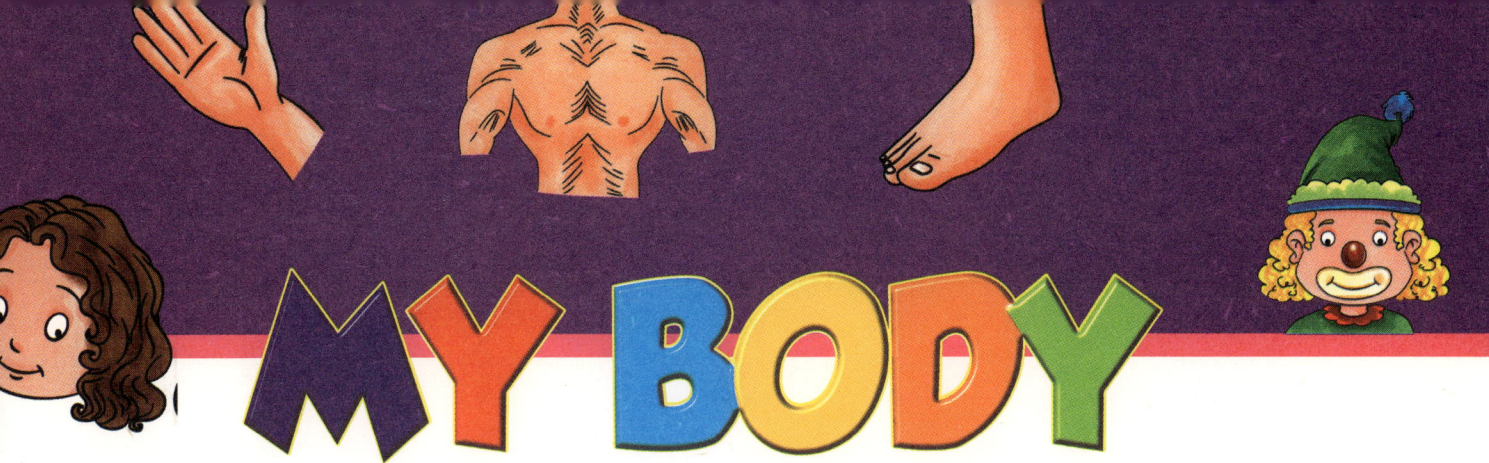

MY BODY

Kiran Rekha Banerji

RED TURTLE
RUPA

Published in Red Turtle by
Rupa Publications India Pvt. Ltd 2017
7/16, Ansari Road, Daryaganj
New Delhi 110002

Sales centres:
Allahabad Bengaluru Chennai
Hyderabad Jaipur Kathmandu
Kolkata Mumbai

Text Copyright © Kiran Rekha Banerji 2017
Illustrations Copyright © Rupa Publications India Pvt. Ltd 2017
Design by Roy Creation

The views and opinions expressed in this book are the author's own and the facts are as reported by him/her which have been verified to the extent possible, and the publishers are not in any way liable for the same.

ISBN: 978-81-291-4634-2

First impression 2017

10 9 8 7 6 5 4 3 2 1

The moral right of the author has been asserted.

Printed at Shree Maitrey Printech Pvt. Ltd, Noida

This book belongs to:

....

....

Your body is unique as it can do many things at the same time. You can walk, jump, run, climb, sit, stand, roll and do many other things as well.

How are these various activities possible? It is the bones and muscles that help us move. You would also know which parts of your body help you to hear, see, smell, feel and taste. You know the parts that can be seen. What about the things hidden inside our body? Have you wondered where the blood comes from when you get hurt?

Hands and Feet

Press your fingers with your left hand. You will feel something hard. This hard part is bones. Bones keep your hand firm.

Why do your fingers and toes bend only in one direction?

All the many tiny bones that make up your fingers and toes are joined by elastic like ligaments that allow some stretching in only one direction.

You have four fingers and a thumb on each hand. These help you to open and close your palm. There are five toes on each foot. The big toe helps you to balance on your feet, to jump and run.

The hard bones also allow you to produce sound when you clap your hands or stamp your feet.

Activity:1. *Take two of your soft toys and bang them together. No sound is made. Now take two wooden or plastic blocks and do the same. Which of them produced a sound?*

Activity:2. *Please take two sheets of paper. On one sheet stick 2-3 ice cream sticks or spoons. Now try rolling / folding the sheets. You will be able to do so with only the one without sticks. This shows how bones keep our body firm.*

Arms and Legs

Move your hand along one of your arms. You can feel a long hard bone under the skin. Your legs and thighs also have long bones. You can bend and move your arms and legs from elbows or knees. These are called joints.

Activity 1: Check out the joints in your favourite doll or Action figure. See how they can bend their elbow and knees.

Activity 2: *Try out a game of "Twister" bending and twisting all the joints.*

Muscles

You cannot feel your bones directly. You will feel something soft spread over your bones. These are covered with layers of fine sheets called muscles. These layers of muscles protect bones and help them move. Your muscles are attached to your bones with elastic threads called tendons.

Activity: *Fold your arms to show off arm muscles like superman/superwoman.*

11

Skin

You are able to feel the difference between hot and cold objects when you touch something. This ability to feel objects is known as the sense of touch. Our skin is a sense organ. It is stretched all over our body and protects our internal organs from harm and diseases. Do you know skin is the largest organ in the human body!

Skin also helps to regulate your body temperature.

Activity: *Touch an ice cube and a mug of hot milk. Now touch them with a cloth. You cannot feel the same sensations because your skin is not touching the objects. What difference did you feel?*

Ears

You hear sounds all the time! How do you hear them? You hear with your ears. Your ears hear different sounds around you. Your brain helps you to understand them. Loud sounds can damage your ears.

Your ears also help you to balance yourself! If you did not have ears you would not be able to stand straight and walk!

What happens when you put your fingers in your ears? Will you hear anything? Find out.

Do you know animals can hear sounds that we cannot hear!

Activity: *You are in a park. What different sounds do you hear? Talk to your parents about them.*

Eyes

Eyes let you see wonderful things around you. They show you objects, colours, shapes and much more. Eyes are the sense organs of sight.

Eyelids cover the eyes. They protect the eye. Eyelids open and shut several times each day in a process called blinking. Touch your eyelids gently; you will feel fine hair called eyelashes. They also help to protect your eyes.

Activity: You are sitting in a park. There are many things around you. Make a list of all that you can see.

Nose

Your nose is placed in the middle of your face. It helps you to breathe. It is also an important organ that allows you to smell.

Your nose has a layer of very tiny hair inside it. When dust enters your nose these hair make you sneeze and throw it out. In this manner, your nose protects your body. Do you know dogs can recognize people just by smelling!

Activity: Some smells are good and some are bad. Name two smells you like and two you don't like.

Tongue

You have a pink tongue inside your mouth. It helps you to talk. It also helps you know if the food you are eating is tasty or not. The tongue has hundreds of tiny taste buds that tell you the taste. Your tongue also helps you eat by moving the food around your mouth.

Activity: *Give the child a few items of food to taste. You can ask what is the difference in their taste. You can also help the child to identify the different tastes associated with the different food items.*

Mouth

You have a mouth that can open and close when you want to speak, sing a song or eat. Lips, teeth and tongue are parts of your mouth. The lips act as guards to protect the mouth. Your lips are soft and pink. You can also make funny faces by moving and curling your lips. Your teeth help you to chew your food.

Activity: *See how your mouth moves when you try blowing, whistling, pressing your lips together, smiling or opening your mouth wide to scream.*

Teeth

The mouth also has a set of lovely white teeth. These help you to bite and chew your food so that it goes down fast to the stomach. You must brush your teeth every morning and night so that they remain healthy. As you grow, the teeth will fall one by one and a new set of stronger teeth will come up.

Do you know a baby has no teeth!

Activity: *Ask your friend to open her mouth. Look at the teeth inside. Do all of them have the same shape?*

Head and Hair

The head is the topmost part of your body. When you touch your head you can feel that it is hard under the skin. The head is made of very strong bones joined together to form the skull. It protects the brain within. Your face is part of your head. The head is protected by hair. Hair acts like a cushion for your head and also keeps it warm. The head rests on your neck. The neck joins your head to your body.

Activity: *Look at these heads and name them.*

Heart and Blood

If you get hurt or cut yourself, you will see a red-coloured liquid come out. This liquid is called blood. Blood flows in every part of our body.

How does the blood reach everywhere?

We have lots of thin narrow tubes called veins and arteries in our body. The blood flows through them. When you place your hand on the left side of your chest you can hear a 'dhup dhup' and feel some movement too. This is your heart. The heart pumps blood so that it reaches all your body parts. Do you know your heart is the size of your fist!

Activity: Take a bottle of squeezy ketchup and press it. Each time you press it, some ketchup comes out. This is the way the heart pumps out blood.

Match the body parts with the pictures.

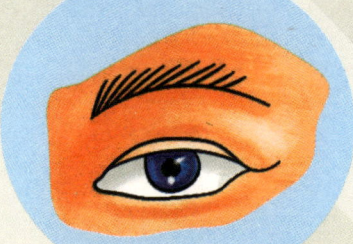

Ear

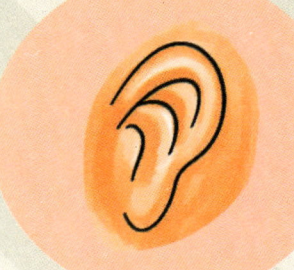

Nose

Eye

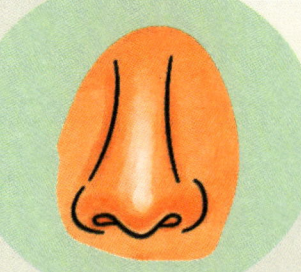

Head

Face

Hand

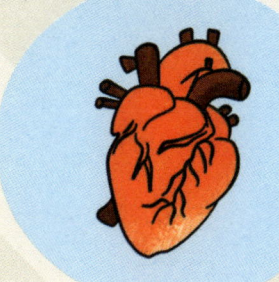

Foot

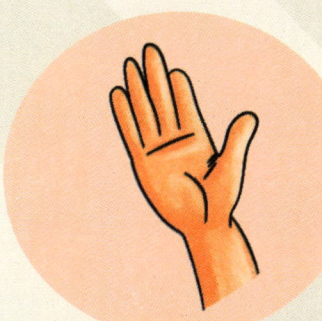

Tongue

Heart

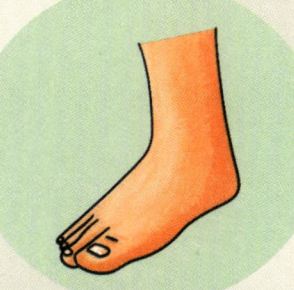

Teeth

What can you do with these parts of your body? Read carefully and write.

hear, smell, touch, taste, see

1. I can _____ with my eye.

2. I can _____ with my ears.

3. I can _____ with my hands.

4. I can _____ with my nose.

5. I can _____ with my tongue.